# The Sophia of Jesus Christ

*Revealing Divine Wisdom and Spiritual Enlightenment*

**A Modern Translation**

Adapted for the Contemporary Reader

**Jesus Christ
(Gnostic Tradition)**

Translated by Tim Zengerink

© **Copyright 2025**
**All rights reserved.**

It is not legal to reproduce, duplicate, or transmit any part of this document in either electronic means or in printed format. Recording of this publication is strictly prohibited and any storage of this document is not allowed unless with written permission from the publisher except for the use of brief quotations in a book review.

This book contains works of fiction. Any resemblance to persons living or dead, or places, events, or locations is purely coincidental.

# Table Of Contents

Preface - Message to the Reader ....................................... 1

Introduction ........................................................................ 5

Sophia of Jesus Christ ..................................................... 11

Thank You for Reading .................................................... 26

# Preface - Message to the Reader

**What If You Could Help Rebuild the Greatest Library in Human History?**

Thousands of years ago, the Library of Alexandria stood as the crown jewel of human achievement — a sanctuary where the collected wisdom of every known civilization was gathered, preserved, and shared freely.

And then, it was lost.

Through fire, conquest, and the slow erosion of time, humanity lost not just books — but ideas, dreams, discoveries, and stories that could have changed the world forever.

Today, the Library of Alexandria lives again — and you are invited to be a part of its restoration.

Our mission is simple yet profound:

**To rebuild the greatest library the world has ever known, and to translate all timeless works into every language and dialect, so that no seeker of knowledge is ever left behind again.**

By joining our movement to rebuild the modern Library of Alexandria, you become part of an unprecedented mission:

- **Unlimited Access to the Greatest Audiobooks & eBooks Ever Written:**

    Instantly explore thousands of legendary works—Plato, Shakespeare, Jane Austen, Leo Tolstoy, and countless more. All instantly available to read or listen, placing a complete literary universe at your fingertips.

- **Beautiful Paperback & Deluxe Editions at Printing Cost**

    Own any title as an elegant paperback, deluxe hardcover, or stunning collectible boxset—offered to you at true printing cost, delivered straight to your door. Build your personal Library of Alexandria, crafted for beauty, built for durability, and worthy of proud display.

- **Fresh Translations for Modern Readers—in Every Language & Dialect**

    Enjoy timeless masterpieces reimagined in clear, contemporary language—no more outdated phrases or obscure references. Alongside the original versions, we're tirelessly translating these classics into every language and dialect imaginable, ensuring accessibility and understanding across cultures and generations.

- **Join a Global Renaissance of Literature & Knowledge**

    You directly support expanding our library, publishing deluxe editions at true cost, translating works into all global languages, and bringing humanity's greatest stories to people everywhere. By joining today, you're not just preserving a legacy of masterpieces; you set in motion a powerful wave of literary accessibility.

**Become a Torchbearer of Knowledge.**

Join us for free now at **LibraryofAlexandria.com**

Together, we will ensure that the light of human wisdom never fades again.

With gratitude and a shared love of knowledge,

The Modern Library of Alexandria Team

Visit:

www.libraryofalexandria.com

Or scan the code below:

# Introduction

## Wisdom as Revelation: The Heart of Gnostic Teaching

The Sophia of Jesus Christ is one of the most luminous and intellectually rich texts in the Gnostic tradition. Discovered among the Nag Hammadi manuscripts and preserved in both Coptic and Greek fragments, this profound dialogue presents the risen Jesus imparting divine wisdom to his disciples. The word "Sophia"—Greek for wisdom—is more than a theological concept in this work; it is a spiritual presence, an active principle of divine truth, and the foundation of all enlightenment. To read this gospel is not merely to learn teachings—it is to encounter the path of illumination.

The dialogue takes place after the resurrection, in a moment of quiet and sacred intimacy. The disciples, overwhelmed by mystery and longing for clarity, ask Jesus to reveal the truths that lie beyond the veil of the physical world. They do not seek history or moral rules—they seek understanding: What is the nature of the divine? What is the origin of the cosmos? Why do souls suffer? And how can one be liberated from the constraints of the material world? Jesus answers not with parables or commandments, but with metaphysical revelation—a vision of reality that encompasses the fullness of being, the descent of the soul, and the journey back to divine unity.

Central to this vision is the figure of Sophia, or divine Wisdom. Sophia is not merely personified as a character but is portrayed as the creative and redemptive force that bridges the gap between the unknowable source and the manifest world. In Gnostic cosmology, Sophia represents both the yearning of the divine to express itself and the misstep that results in the formation of a flawed, ignorant world. Her fall—an act of independent creation outside the fullness of divine will—leads to the birth of the Demiurge, the architect of the material universe. This myth does not condemn Sophia but venerates her as the mother of spiritual striving. She suffers, descends, and calls the soul upward. Her story is our story: the drama of seeking, forgetting, and remembering.

In Jesus' teachings, Sophia is also the one who makes knowledge possible. Without her, there is no gnosis—no revelation of the hidden truths that can set the soul free. She is not a doctrine but a presence that must be recognized within. Her wisdom is not imparted from above but awakened from within. To know Sophia is to know oneself, and to know oneself is to remember the divine origin obscured by the illusions of the world.

This gospel makes clear that salvation is not achieved through belief alone, but through self-knowledge. The one who knows the truth of their own being—the divine spark hidden within the soul—can transcend the powers of the material world and ascend through the spiritual realms. This ascent is not merely an afterlife promise but a present reality. It begins with awareness, matures through inner work, and culminates in union with the source.

## The Divine Structure of Reality and the Call to Awakening

The cosmology presented in The Sophia of Jesus Christ is vast and intricately ordered. It speaks of the ineffable Father—the invisible, boundless One who cannot be named or defined. From this source emanate a series of divine beings known as aeons, each expressing a different aspect of the fullness (pleroma). These aeons do not exist in time or space but represent qualities of divine mind: thought, will, grace, truth, and wisdom. Sophia is the last of these aeons, and her journey into separation initiates the drama of creation.

Sophia's action—creating without her consort—results in the emergence of the Demiurge, a blind and arrogant being who fashions the material world, believing himself to be the only god. This being, identified with the god of Genesis in some Gnostic readings, is not evil by nature but profoundly ignorant. He is unaware of the higher realities and imposes his flawed creation upon the soul. His world is filled with suffering, injustice, and fragmentation. Yet even here, the divine spark persists—planted in humanity by Sophia and sustained by the hidden presence of the true Light.

Jesus explains that humanity is caught in this in-between state: divine by nature, yet imprisoned by forgetfulness. The journey of the soul, then, is a process of awakening—not of acquiring something new, but of remembering what was always true. This awakening requires resistance to the external authorities of the world—the archons, or rulers, who govern through fear, desire, and deception. These figures, both literal and symbolic, represent the forces that pull us away from our divine origin and obscure the truth of who we are.

The gospel emphasizes the role of the revealer—Jesus—as the one who descends into the world not to condemn, but to remind. He is the Logos, the divine Word, who speaks what cannot otherwise be known. He is the embodiment of divine wisdom, come to awaken Sophia within each soul. His teachings are not about obedience to religious law, but about liberation from inner darkness. He invites the disciples, and all who hear his voice, to enter into the mystery—not by following rules, but by becoming fully alive in spirit.

In this way, The Sophia of Jesus Christ is both cosmological and existential. It maps the structure of reality, but it also maps the interior of the soul. It describes divine hierarchies, but its true concern is transformation. It teaches that every human being carries the image of the divine and that enlightenment is not a reward for the few, but the birthright of all who seek. The path is not external—it is inward. It is not about separation from the world, but about seeing through it to the truth that sustains it.

This modern translation has been prepared to bring the full depth, beauty, and clarity of this ancient text to contemporary readers. Archaic terminology has been refined, obscure symbols clarified, and dense metaphysics rendered in language that invites reflection and resonance. Yet the integrity of the original has been preserved: its rhythm, its mystery, and its spiritual intensity remain intact.

To read The Sophia of Jesus Christ is to receive an invitation—not to adopt a new belief, but to awaken to a deeper reality. It is to encounter the divine not as an abstract force, but as an inner presence. It is to understand that true wisdom is not something to be given or taken, but something to be recognized in silence, in stillness, in truth.

Let this gospel be your guide through the layers of illusion. Let Sophia speak to you—not as a character, but as a living truth. Let Jesus' voice awaken in you the memory of who you are and where you came from. And may this journey lead you not only to knowledge, but to the peace and clarity that come from knowing the divine wisdom that dwells within.

# Sophia of Jesus Christ

After Jesus rose from the dead, his twelve disciples and seven women followers stayed faithful to him. They traveled to Galilee, to a mountain called "Divination and Joy." While they were there, they were filled with questions. They wanted to understand the truth about the universe, God's plan, the power of the rulers, and everything the Savior had been teaching them about the mysteries of the divine.

Then, the Savior appeared to them—not in the physical form they had known before, but as a shining, invisible spirit. His presence was as bright as a great angel of light. I cannot describe exactly how he looked because no human body could handle such a sight. Only a pure and perfected body, like the one he had told us about on the mountain called "Of the Olives" in Galilee, could see him fully.

He greeted them, saying, "Peace be with you. My peace I give to you." At his words, they were filled with awe and fear. Seeing this, the Savior laughed softly and said, "Why are you confused? What are you thinking? What are you searching for?"

Philip spoke up and said, "We want to understand the truth about the universe and God's plan."

The Savior replied, "Listen carefully. Every person who has ever lived on this earth, from the beginning of time until now, is made of dust. Many have searched for God, trying to understand who he is and what he is like, but they have not been able to find him. Even the wisest people have only made guesses about him by watching the world and how it moves. But their guesses have not led them to the truth.

"Philosophers have three different ideas about how the world is governed, but they do not agree with each other. Some say the world controls itself. Others believe it is guided by a higher power. Some think that everything is ruled by fate. But none of these ideas are true. They are only human thoughts, not the real answer.

"But I have come from the Infinite Light, and I know the truth. That is why I am here—to tell you what is real. Anything that exists by itself is weak and will eventually fall apart because it was made without wisdom. What people call 'providence' has no true knowledge, and what they call 'fate' has no understanding. But you have been chosen to know the truth. Those who are worthy of knowledge will receive it—not those born from unclean acts, but those born from the One who was sent by the First. That One is immortal among mortals."

Matthew then said, "Lord, no one can find the truth except through you. Please teach us what is real."

The Savior replied, "The One Who Truly Exists cannot be fully described. No ruler, no power, no authority, and no created being has ever known him completely—not from the beginning of time until now. Only he knows himself, and he reveals himself only through the One who came from the First Light.

"From now on, I am the Great Savior. He is immortal and eternal—he was never born and will never die. Anything that is born will one day come to an end. He has no beginning because anything that has a beginning must also have an end. Since no one created him, no one rules over him. He has no name, because anything with a name was given that name by someone else."

Jesus continued, "He has no name because anything with a name was given one by someone else. He has no human form because anything that has a human shape was created by another. His appearance is beyond anything you have seen or could imagine. He is greater than all things, greater than the universe itself. He sees himself in all directions and reflects upon himself. Because he has no limits, he cannot be fully understood. He is eternal and unchanging, perfect in every way. No one can measure him or trace his existence, yet he completely knows himself, even though he remains unknown to others. He is called the 'Father of the Universe.'"

Philip then asked, "Lord, how does he reveal himself to those who are perfect?"

The Savior replied, "Before anything in the visible world existed, his greatness and authority were already present. He holds everything within himself, but nothing holds him. He is pure thought, understanding, wisdom, reason, and power—all of these exist equally within him. They are the source of all things. Everything that has ever existed or ever will exist was already known by him, the one who has no beginning."

Thomas then asked, "Lord, why did all these things come into existence? Why were they made known?"

The Savior answered, "I came from the Infinite to explain this to you. The Spirit that has always existed was the source of creation. It had the power to shape all things and bring life into being. This happened so that the great goodness within him could be shared. Out of his love and kindness, he did not want to keep this goodness to himself, but he wanted others to experience it. That is why he brought forth eternal beings—so they could create, bring forth life, and give glory and honor. In this way, his endless love and grace could be revealed.

"The Self-Begotten God, the source of all things that never perish, revealed this treasure. However, even though these creations existed, they were not yet visible. There is a great difference between things that last forever and things that will eventually pass away."

Then he said, "Whoever is ready to understand these mysteries, let them listen!" And he added, "I speak to those who are awake."

He continued, "Everything that comes from something temporary will one day disappear because it came from something that does not last. But whatever comes from what is eternal will never perish and will remain forever. Many people have been misled because they did not understand this difference, and because of this, they have died."

Mary asked, "Lord, how can we recognize this truth?"

The Savior replied, "Move from what is invisible to what is visible. If you follow this path, the understanding of true knowledge will become clear, and you will see that even in the visible world, there is faith in the unseen. These things belong to the One Who Has No Beginning. Whoever is ready to hear this, let them listen!

"The Lord of the Universe is not just called 'Father' but 'Forefather,' the source of all that has appeared. Yet, he himself has no beginning. When he looked within himself, he saw his own reflection, like a mirror. Through this, he appeared in a form like himself. This revealed his Divine Self—the First, the One Who Has No Beginning. Though he exists alongside the eternal Light that came before him, he is not equal to it in power.

"After this, a vast number of self-created beings appeared, all equal in age and power, shining in glorious light beyond counting. This group is called 'The Generation That Has No Ruler.' You are part of them. They are known as 'Children of the Unbegotten Father, God, Savior, Son of God,' whose image is also within you. He is beyond understanding, filled with everlasting glory and endless joy. All these beings find peace in him, celebrating his unchanging greatness and limitless happiness. Until now, this truth had never been known or spoken of in all the realms and worlds that exist."

Matthew asked, "Lord, how was humanity created?"

Jesus answered, "I want you to understand that before anything existed, beyond all limits, there was the Self-Created Father, full of light and beyond description. When he chose to reveal himself, his first great power appeared as the Immortal Androgynous Man. This

Immortal Man was meant to bring salvation and awaken others from their ignorance, guiding them until the struggle against darkness is over.

"His partner is the Great Sophia, who was always meant to be with him, as planned by the Self-Existing Father. From the Immortal Man came divinity, the kingdom, and the first revelation of the Father, who is called 'Man, Self-Father.' The Father created a vast eternal realm, called 'Ogdoad,' to reflect his own greatness.

"The Immortal Man was given great authority over the lower world, which was lacking in spiritual wealth. He created gods, angels, and rulers—countless beings to serve him. They were brought into existence from his Light and from the triple-male Spirit, which belonged to his partner, Sophia. From them, divinity and kingship came into being, which is why he is called the 'God of gods' and the 'King of kings.'

"The First Man contains wisdom, thought, reflection, reason, and power within himself. He is not separate from these qualities; they are part of him. All these traits are perfect and eternal. They are equal in being imperishable, but they differ in power—just as a father differs from his son, and a son from his thoughts, and thoughts from what they create. As I have told you before, the first source of all things is the monad.

"From the monad, all things came into existence through his power. What was created gave rise to what was formed, and what was formed was given a name. This is how everything unfolded, from the beginning to the end."

Bartholomew then asked, "Why is he called 'Man' and 'Son of Man' in the Gospel? Who is this Son connected to?"

Jesus answered, "The First Man is called the 'Begetter, Self-Perfected Mind.' With his partner, Great Sophia, he brought forth his first-born, an androgynous child. His male name is 'First Begetter, Son of God,' and his female name is 'First Begettress Sophia, Mother of the Universe.' Some also call her 'Love.' This First-Born is known as 'Christ.' Since he inherited authority from his Father, he created countless angels from Spirit and Light to serve as his messengers."

The disciples then asked, "Lord, please tell us more about the one called 'Man,' so we can fully understand his greatness."

Jesus replied, "Whoever is ready to understand, let them listen carefully. The First Father is also called 'Adam, Eye of Light' because he comes from the radiant Light. His holy angels, who are beyond description and cast no shadows, rejoice forever in the reflection of their Father. The entire kingdom of the Son of Man, also known as the 'Son of God,' shares in this joy. Their never-ending happiness reflects his eternal glory—a glory that had never been revealed in all the realms and worlds that came afterward. I have come from the Self-Existing One and the First Infinite Light to bring you these truths."

The disciples then asked, "Tell us clearly how they came down from the invisible, immortal realm into this world of death."

Jesus explained, "The Son of Man joined with his partner, Sophia, and together they revealed a great androgynous Light. His male name is 'Savior, Creator of All Things,' and his female name is 'All-Creating Sophia.' Some also call her 'Pistis.'"

Everyone who comes into the world is like a drop of Light, sent by Him to the world ruled by the Almighty so they can be protected. However, they are placed under the power of forgetfulness, as Sophia intended. This forgetfulness exists so that the world can see the arrogance, blindness, and ignorance of the Almighty. But I came from the higher realms, sent by the Great Light. I escaped from this forgetfulness, broke the hold of the false rulers, and awakened the drop of Light sent from Sophia so it could grow and bear much fruit through me. It was made perfect so it would never fall into imperfection again but would instead unite with me, the Great Savior, and reveal His glory. Through this, Sophia would be justified, ensuring that her children would no longer be trapped in failure. Instead, they would receive honor, return to their Father, and understand the words of the Masculine Light.

You were sent by the Son, who was sent so that you might receive the Light and free yourselves from the forgetfulness created by the rulers. You must never allow this forgetfulness to return. It came from the unclean mixture of fearful fire, which arose from their physical nature. You must reject their corrupt intentions and rise above them.

Then Thomas asked, "Lord, how many realms exist above the heavens?"

Jesus answered, "I am pleased that you ask about the great realms, for your origins are in the infinite. When those I spoke of earlier were revealed, the Self-Existing Father created twelve realms for the twelve angels, giving them perfect and pure companions. This act made the flaw in the female clear."

He continued, "Whoever is ready to understand, let them listen. The first realm belongs to the Son of Man, known as the 'First Begetter' and 'Savior,' who has now appeared. The second realm belongs to Man, called 'Adam, Eye of Light.' Above both of these is the greatest realm, beyond all kingdoms, which belongs to the Eternal Infinite God, the Self-Existing Source of all realms. This includes the immortals I spoke of earlier. It is above the Seventh and appeared from Sophia, the first realm.

"The Immortal Man revealed realms, powers, and kingdoms, granting authority to all who appeared within Him. These beings acted according to their will until everything above chaos was revealed. They worked together to create magnificent things, including many radiant and endless lights. These lights, filled with indescribable glory, were called the first, second, and third realms. The first is known as 'Unity and Rest.' Each realm was given its own name. The third realm is called 'Assembly,' representing the gathering of many into one. This Assembly, also known as the 'Assembly of the Eighth,' appeared as both male and female. The male aspect is called 'Assembly,' and the female aspect is called 'Life,' because life for all the realms came through a female. From the beginning, everything was named in order.

"Through the power and thoughts of these beings, others appeared who were called 'gods.' From their wisdom, these gods created more gods. From these gods came lords, and from the thoughts of the lords, more lords appeared. From the lords' power, archangels were formed. The words of the archangels brought forth angels. From these angels, all things—structures, shapes, and forms—came into existence, each with its own name for all the realms and their worlds.

"The immortals I just described received their authority from the Immortal Man, who is also called 'Silence.' Through her silent reflection, her own greatness was made complete. The imperishable ones, having this authority, each created a great kingdom in the Eighth realm. They built thrones, temples, and heavens to reflect their glory. All of this was done according to the will of the Mother of the Universe."

The apostles said, "Lord, please tell us more about the beings who exist in the higher realms. We want to understand them better."

Jesus answered, "If you ask, I will explain. These beings created countless angels to serve them and reflect their glory. They also created pure spirits—lights that never weaken or suffer. These lights exist through will alone and came into being instantly.

"In this way, the higher realms were completed, along with the heavens and their foundations, all reflecting the greatness of the Immortal Man and Sophia, His companion. From this perfection, every realm and world took its pattern for creation. Even the lower chaotic realms followed these patterns. From the beginning of chaos, everything has existed in Light, shining without shadow. The beings there live in indescribable joy, always celebrating their unchanging glory. No other realms or rulers can compare. I have told you all this so you may shine in the Light beyond all these worlds."

Mary asked, "Lord, where do your disciples come from, and where are they going? What is their purpose here?"

Jesus replied, "Sophia, the Mother of the Universe, wanted to create on her own, without her male counterpart. But by the will of the true Father, His boundless goodness was revealed. He created a division between the immortal beings and those who came later. This separation allowed the imperfection in the female to appear, and Error arose to challenge her. This became the spiritual barrier.

"From the higher realms, Light descended into the lower chaotic worlds like drops of Light and Spirit. These drops took form within chaos, bringing judgment upon the false creator, Yaldabaoth. These forms, given breath, became living souls. But they were weak and trapped in ignorance. Only when the Great Light of the Male touched them did they awaken and receive names. By the will of Sophia, Immortal Man began gathering the elements to bring judgment on the false rulers.

"The beings of chaos were like souls, but they could not understand true power until the time of chaos ended, as set by the great angel. I have taught you about Immortal Man and freed Him from the grip of the false rulers. I broke the gates of those who show no mercy and exposed their evil. Their arrogance was humbled, and their ignorance was defeated. This is why I came—to reconnect these beings with Spirit and Breath, restoring them to their original unity. By doing this, you will produce much fruit and rise to the One Who Has Always Been, experiencing unshakable joy, glory, and grace from the Father of the Universe."

Whoever truly knows the Father through pure understanding will return to Him and find peace in the Eternal One. But those who only know Him imperfectly will remain in the Eighth realm. Those who understand the Immortal Spirit through silence, deep thought, and truth must show me the signs of the Invisible One, and they will become a light in the Spirit of Silence. Those who know the Son of Man through wisdom and love must show me the signs of the Son of Man so they may live in the Eighth realm.

I have revealed to you the name of the Perfect One and the will of the Mother of the Holy Angels. Because of this, the divine realm will be completed, appearing in the higher worlds and spreading throughout the boundless riches of the Great Invisible Spirit. All beings will receive from His goodness, even the eternal peace that no kingdom can control. I came from the First One Sent so I could reveal to you the One Who Exists from the Beginning. I have done this to expose the arrogance of the false rulers who claim to be gods. I came to remove their blindness and show the world the true God, who is above everything.

Therefore, rise up against their lies, expose their deception, and break the chains they place on others. Awaken those who belong to me. I have given you power over all things as Sons of Light so you may walk over their false authority without fear.

These are the words the blessed Savior spoke before disappearing from their sight. After this, the disciples were filled with overwhelming joy in the Spirit. They went out to share the message of God, the eternal and unchanging Light. Amen.

# Thank You for Reading

Dear Reader,

We hope this timeless classic has sparked your imagination and enriched your literary journey. Now that you've turned the final page, we want to share a vision for the future of reading—one where every classic you've ever wanted to explore is at your fingertips, in a format that best suits your life.

We'd like to invite you to gain immediate, unlimited digital & audiobook access to hundreds of the most treasured literary classics ever written—along with the option to secure deluxe paperback, hardcover & box set editions at printing cost. Together, we can spark a new global literary renaissance alongside our small, independent publishing house called "The Library of Alexandria."

Thousands of years ago, the Library of Alexandria stood as a beacon of knowledge—until it was lost to history. We aim to reignite that spirit of preservation and discovery right now, in the modern age—only this time, it's accessible to all, in every language and every format.

Picture a world where every timeless classic, novel, poem, or philosophical treatise is not only available to read but also updated for today's readers—modernized, translated into any language or dialect, and ready to enjoy in any format you choose, whether that is in an eBook, audiobook, paperback, or deluxe hardcover & box set version a printing cost.

By joining our movement to rebuild the modern Library of Alexandria, you become part of an unprecedented mission to offer:

- **Unlimited Audiobook & eBook Access to the Greatest Classics of All Time**

    Instantly explore thousands of legendary works, from Plato and Shakespeare to Jane Austen and Leo Tolstoy. All are instantly ready to read or listen to, giving you a complete literary universe at your fingertips.

- **Paperback & Deluxe Editions at Printing Costs:**

    Purchase any title in a paperback, deluxe hardbound, or deluxe boxset edition at printing costs, shipped right to your doorstep. Curate your personal library of Alexandria with editions worthy of display—crafted to last, designed to captivate, and delivered straight to your door.

- **Modern translations for Contemporary Readers in all languages and dialects**

  Discover a vast selection of classics reimagined in clear, current language—no more struggling with outdated phrases or obscure references. Next to the original versions, we aim to offer translations in as many languages and dialects as possible.

  As we continue our translation efforts and add new languages, readers everywhere can connect with these works as if they were written today. By bridging linguistic divides, you're contributing to ensuring that these timeless stories become more meaningful, accessible, and inspiring for people across the globe.

- **Your Personal Library of Alexandria:**

  Over the months and years, you'll curate a unique physical archive of classics—each volume a testament to your taste, curiosity, and love of knowledge. It's not just about owning books—it's about curating a cultural legacy you'll cherish and pass down for generations to come.

- **Join a Global Literary Renaissance:**

  Your support fuels an ongoing mission: allowing us to reinvest in offering deluxe print editions (including special boxsets) at their true cost, broaden the range of available formats and translations, and extend the reach of these works to new audiences worldwide. By joining today, you're not just preserving a legacy of masterpieces; you set in motion a powerful wave of literary accessibility.

We are more than a publisher—we're a movement, and we can't do it alone. Your support lets us scale our mission, preserving and reimagining history's greatest works for tomorrow's readers.

**Become a Torchbearer of knowledge.**

Thank you for picking up this book and allowing us into your literary journey. As you turn the pages, know that you're part of something larger: a global effort to keep these stories alive, share their wisdom across borders and generations, and spark a true cultural revival for the modern era.

If this resonates with you—please consider taking the next step by visiting:

**www.libraryofalexandria.com**

With gratitude and a shared love of knowledge,

*The Modern Library of Alexandria Team*

Visit:

www.libraryofalexandria.com

Or scan the code below:

www.ingramcontent.com/pod-product-compliance
Lightning Source LLC
LaVergne TN
LVHW030631080426
835512LV00021B/3465